T0370528

Finding Hope: Reflections on Gratitude, Faith, and Resilience

DR. A. LaSharnda Beckwith

authorHOUSE

AuthorHouse™
1663 Liberty Drive
Bloomington, IN 47403
www.authorhouse.com
Phone: 833-262-8899

Published by AuthorHouse 10/17/2024

ISBN: 979-8-8230-3228-5 (sc)
ISBN: 979-8-8230-3229-2 (hc)
ISBN: 979-8-8230-3227-8 (e)

Library of Congress Control Number: 2024917014

Print information available on the last page.

This book is printed on acid-free paper.

FOREWORD

It's been said that the depression of our age is learned helplessness. Far too many feel they are powerless to make a difference in what happens to them. Hope is elusive for far too many. Just know that help is on the way. I've seen Dr. LaSharnda Beckwith live the principles she reveals in this amazing book. She doesn't just find hope. She claims it, embraces it, and uses it to empower her life and serve others. She wants you to do the same. This book gives you a ready road map to faith and hope that can endure and help you daily to live the life you desire.

It's an honest book that confronts the problems and realities most of us experience. We've all had relationships that could be described more as a betrayal than a reliable supporter. We've felt alone and sure that others would soon find out that we are imposters incapable of doing what other successful people do. Dr. Beckwith has had her own challenges facing rejection, setbacks, unreliable "friends," and doubts of her own. We don't need perfect people to tell us how imperfect we know we already are. We need wisdom from people who have lived through what we now face and succeeded anyway with the help of faith in God, a thankful attitude, and a resilience earned through overcoming obstacle after obstacle. This book not only shares what has worked for Dr. Beckwith, but she also challenges you to reflect on the insights shared and take what fits for you. This is your journey. You will know what works for you. Claim it, and then get busy making those insights and truths your own.

I've known Dr. Beckwith for eight years. As board chair of Lutheran Social Services of Southern California for eight years, I was blessed to be leader of the board that hired Dr. Beckwith as our CEO. From the beginning, we knew we had made the right choice. She seizes the day with anticipation, is grateful for what comes, knows God is her anchor, and is ready to bounce back from any setback that comes her way and take her team with her. After reading this book and internalizing the powerful insights shared, you will be inspired to do the same with your life. As a PhD psychologist and author of *The Optimism Advantage*, I know you will enjoy this insightful window into hope and happiness. Seize this book, devour it, and then live it. Do that, and others will notice the difference—and so will you. Thank you, Dr. Beckwith, for this powerful window into claiming our own hope and vital faith.

Terry Paulson, PhD
Psychologist, author, and speaker on making change work and former chair of the board for Lutheran Social Services of Southern California

1

Faith and Optimism: Navigating Uncertain Times with Hope

I am sure you never thought we would experience a pandemic in our lifetime. However, now we have. Not only has the world dealt with the ramifications of the recent pandemic, but we have also watched a stabilized nation become destabilized and people who were living everyday lives suddenly displaced.

I don't know about you, but if I wasn't so focused on being optimistic about the future, I could find myself in a place of despair. From 2020 until now, I can count the various things that could cause people to want to give up. I want to encourage you to hold on, have faith, trust God, and believe times will change for the better. Is that pie in the sky? Maybe. I intend always to offer hope because my faith demands it.

One of my favorite scriptures encourages just that: to have faith. I know times have been hard. We have been challenged repeatedly over the years but cannot give up if we want to live full lives again. Do you? I do. If I live here on this earth, I intend to live life to the fullest. When there was a window to travel, I did. When I had the opportunity to go out and eat dinner with friends, I have, and when I could go to a store, spa, or office, I was thrilled to do so. Because we need each other, and isolation helps no one. I believe isolation sets up the environment for emotional and mental harm. I love my solitude, but I also recognize the dangers of too much isolation. It is easy to fall into dark spaces when no outside voice reminds you of your goodness. Sometimes we need to be reminded of the possibilities and look forward to a better and brighter tomorrow.

Oprah Winfrey said, "When I look into the future, it's so bright it burns my eyes." That is what we have had to remember during days of chaos. We must remind ourselves of the happy days ahead, whether we see them or not, and believe they are there. Never forget that we are what we think; what we think begins with what we allow our minds to consume. To ensure our minds are optimistic, we must be selective and intentional. How can we ensure we have the correct thinking? Look to the scriptures.

Philippians 4:8 says, "Finally, brothers, whatever is true, whatever is honorable, whatever is right, whatever is pure, whatever is lovely, whatever is admirable—if anything is excellent or praiseworthy—think on these things."

I don't know about you, but I believe the future is so bright, it hurts my eyes!

Reflection:

_____

_____

_____

_____

_____

_____

_____

_____

_____

_____

_____

_____

_____

_____

_____

_____

_____

_____

_____

_____

_____

_____

2

Believe in Yourself: A Story of Resilience and Triumph

Have you ever heard the phrase "If not now, when? If not you, who?" I have always liked that saying because it epitomizes how I have lived my life. I have always believed that I could either sit around and blame someone else for my challenges, make excuses for why I could not do something, wait for someone to give me a chance or not give me one, or plot my path.

I was excited and enthusiastic about everything when I began my work career. I remember the first time I interviewed for the management training program with the Army & Air Force Exchange Service. That program offered college graduates an opportunity to join the company at the lowest managerial level and learn to be a manager. I recall the interview in Dallas and visiting the headquarters building. I was so enamored with the various professionals walking around, and back then, people wore suits to work!

Being from a family of churchgoers and not white-collar professionals, I always knew this was the kind of person I wanted to be. So although I was not a student anyone took an interest in, except one female basketball coach who also inspired me, I had to learn to believe in myself. I remember just being happy to be there with all the other potential hires. After the interviews, I got on the plane back to Florida, praying that

I would be offered a job. Every day, I waited for the mail to see if I would receive a positive response from the company. Finally, one day, it came, and I was so happy to be seen, believed in, and accepted as a person for their program.

Today, some might think that my life's journey has been easy and I had only wonderful moments with no challenges at all. I was the first one in my family to attend college and graduate. When I told my family members I wanted to go to college, no one asked why. They just figured out a way for me to go. Their attitude was "Why not her?" and that was my attitude. No one had done it before me, but that didn't mean I couldn't do it! So if not me, who?

After I had finished college, almost every one of my family members who came up after me also attended college. When I started working a white-collar job, nearly every family member younger than me did so also. Why? It's because they saw it to be possible.

Today is a new day. Don't allow people with bad attitudes and old grudges to keep you from your dreams. Stop listening to the chatter of why you cannot do something. When others begin to project on you their limitations, don't accept them. When they say that the system isn't for you, challenge the system. Not in a hostile or aggressive way but in a positive, polished, self-assured manner. Let your attitude be one of the possibilities, not problems. Tell yourself and others, "If not now, when? If not me, who?" and let them try to convince you otherwise!

Reflection:

_____

_____

_____

_____

_____

_____

_____

_____

_____

_____

_____

_____

_____

_____

_____

_____

_____

_____

_____

_____

_____

_____

RECOGNIZING SIGNS OF FAKE FRIENDS: TRUSTING YOUR INTUITION

Don't be surprised when people you thought supported you never really did. This type of fake friendship became very clear to me over the years. Although I probably already knew that deep down they did not care for me, I chose to ignore my gut. Anyway, I think we always know whether someone likes us or not. It isn't hard. We know based on their actions or inactions. Yes, we know because our gut or intuition warns us.

Yet it always surprises me when people are shocked that their betrayer finally shows their true face. Honestly, I am never really shocked anymore. When it happens these days, I just go with it. I may be caught off guard for a minute, but I am not astonished that some people I trusted didn't care for me.

What do we do when we feel betrayed? Learn and not blame. Learn from the experience, and do not wallow in self-pity. And don't blame yourself for not seeing it sooner. Also, do not ask yourself, "Why?" or "What did you do?" If you did something, apologize, but more likely than not, you did nothing.

Generally we are raised to give people the benefit of the doubt. When we see signs such as people joking about us, making passive-aggressive comments toward us, etc., our gut warns us, but we tend to ignore it. We don't want to assume bad things about others.

We all do it, so you are with the majority. Although you will play your friendship over the years repeatedly in your mind, trying to look for signs you missed, let that play out. For some reason, we must figure out where we went wrong in judging the fake friend. Finding out that someone you valued never valued you is hard. The sooner you accept that, the sooner the healing process can begin. If you are a believer, turn to scripture and prayer for comfort.

One scripture I found reassured me that God will avenge me if I am confident that I have clean hands and heart. That doesn't mean that I want the person to be held accountable. Not in the least. What I want is for me to move past them as quickly as possible. But if someone goes beyond just hurting your feelings and disparages your name, remember Psalm 101:5–6.

> I will destroy the one who secretly slanders a friend. I will not allow the proud and arrogant to prevail. My eyes are looking at the faithful of the land so that they may live with me; The one who lives a life of integrity will serve me.

See? You don't have to do anything except learn from the experience and not blame yourself. All else God will handle. Keep living, keep loving, and keep an open mind to future friendships. Maybe God is clearing the way for new and better friendships.

Reflection:

_____

_____

_____

_____

_____

_____

_____

_____

_____

_____

_____

_____

_____

_____

_____

_____

_____

_____

_____

_____

_____

3

Understanding Betrayal: A Path to Personal Growth and Healing

Have you ever pondered the enigmatic question "What is it about me?" It's a question that tends to surface when relationships crumble before our eyes, leaving us confused and heartbroken. We wonder why people betray us, and we may even question what could be inherently wrong with us. The quest to understand the root of this issue can be both introspective and revealing.

First and foremost, it's essential to acknowledge that betrayal is a complex and multifaceted aspect of human relationships. It often stems from various factors, such as miscommunication, unmet expectations, and personal insecurities. While it's easy to internalize these experiences and wonder what we did wrong, it's crucial to remember that betrayal does not always reflect our worth or character.

Scripture provides wisdom and comfort during times of personal reflection and adversity. In times of doubt and introspection, we can turn to my favorite book, the Bible. Proverbs 3:5–6 says, "Trust in the Lord with all your heart and lean not to your understanding, in all your ways acknowledge Him, and He will make your path straight." This scripture reminds us that while we may question ourselves and our circumstances, trust in God can provide clarity and guidance.

Self-reflection is an essential step in understanding the dynamics of our relationships. It can help us identify patterns in our interactions with others and reveal areas where we may need personal growth or improvement. However, this should not be a journey of self-blame or self-criticism but an opportunity for self-awareness and self-empowerment.

When you find yourself asking, "What is it about me?" don't just blame yourself for whatever went wrong. Instead, reframe your thoughts and consider the following:

- Misunderstandings can lead to strained relationships. Reflect on your communication style. I didn't say to change it, but consider how you communicate. I know I must do so regularly.
- Unrealistic or unspoken expectations can lead to disappointment and feelings of betrayal.
- Self-esteem and self-worth significantly affect how we perceive and respond to betrayal. I have a strong sense of self, which helps me navigate challenging situations more confidently.
- Betrayal can erode trust, making it difficult to establish healthy connections. I remind myself often that I have trust issues, which causes me to keep my guard up. Consider how trust issues may have affected your relationships and what steps you can take to rebuild trust.
- Use the experience of betrayal as an opportunity for personal growth. Embrace the lessons learned and seek ways to become a better version of yourself.
- Sometimes, seeking guidance from a trusted friend or therapist can provide valuable insights and support in understanding your role in relationships and any recurring patterns.

Remember that relationships are a two-way street. While self-reflection is essential, it's equally important to recognize that betrayal often arises from both parties' complexities. Ultimately, asking, "What is it about me?" can be a catalyst for personal growth and healthier, more fulfilling relationships. It's a question that can lead to self-discovery and a deeper understanding of the intricate dynamics of human connections.

Over the years, I have always had my guard up. People who knew me understood the "guarded me" and just accepted it. There has always been a good reason to guard myself because, true to form, people I would let in would betray me. I would often accept the betrayal as another lesson learned, but sometimes I had to ask myself, "What is it about me?"

Reflection:

_____

_____

_____

_____

_____

_____

_____

_____

_____

_____

_____

_____

_____

_____

_____

_____

_____

_____

4

Coping with Adversity: Embracing Hope and Faith in Challenging Circumstances

I recognize that sickness and death are a part of our life cycle. Nevertheless, when people go through these life-changing events, I am reminded of how precious life is and how grateful I am to be given another day. I also think about the pain and heartbreak those closest to the situation are going through. I would like to know what I can do to ease the pain. When they share their devastating news, what do I say? I understand. We don't if we haven't experienced it, and even if we have, we don't understand their circumstances. Then do we say, "I will be praying for you"? Of course, we will, but more than those praying statements may be needed.

What do we do when we don't know what to do? I can't outline a plan for anyone to follow in such situations. I can only share that I stopped to pray. I pray that God will give me the right words or lead me to be quiet and sit in silence, waiting for Him to lead the way. Sometimes the silence is deafening, and we want to fill the space. But we should not rush to fill the silence; we should let the Holy Spirit do His work at that time.

One of the most effective tools in our arsenal during difficult times can be disconnecting from all the voices and plugging into the one voice that is sometimes drowned out in the chaos. The voice we need to hear the most is the voice of God. I am not saying an audible voice, but the feeling in your soul, whispering, reminding you that you are not alone. Something you read might remind you of your strength, even in your most vulnerable state, because He is with you.

You may feel alone, but you are not alone. You may feel helpless to help someone you love going through something you wish you could change, but you are not weak; you can show them hope. That hope can be shared through your smile, support, or just sitting and listening to another person.

No matter where we find ourselves today, God knows where we are and where we are supposed to be. He will use us during the dark times, just as He does in the good ones. We are His workmanship and vessels; let Him use you regardless of what you are facing.

Reflection:

_____

_____

_____

_____

_____

_____

_____

_____

_____

_____

_____

_____

_____

_____

_____

_____

_____

_____

_____

_____

_____

_____

5

Imposter Syndrome? Grace Transforms Insecurities

I explored a theme that I have heard repeatedly. The term is *imposter syndrome.* After reading about it and hearing comments from various people, I began to wonder about it for myself. Do I ever experience this phenomenon? If I did, would I admit it to anyone? I would admit it to my husband. But in such a competitive world, I can see why people feel they are imposters, especially at work.

Social media doesn't help, either. We believe everything we see on these platforms; worse yet, some of us compare ourselves to others and measure our happiness by their posts. We see friends and family traveling the world, looking happy, only to hear not long after a trip that there is shocking news that life perhaps wasn't as rosy as portrayed. Looking at extremely popular people, we suddenly hear they have decided that life is too hard.

I believe we can all be imposters at some point. However, I would not ascribe that description to many people I know. We are all just trying to do our best. Life gets complicated, and people want not only to survive but also to thrive. So they put on a face, even when the going gets tough, and forge ahead.

If you feel you are an imposter, a person who often wears a mask to conceal your insecurities, join the club. But also know that God knows who we are from the inside out and still loves us. His grace is a mirror reflecting our true worth. I am sure you know this scripture: "For it is by grace you have been saved, through faith—and this is not from yourselves, it is the gift of God—not by works so that no one can boast" (Ephesians 2:8–9). See, there you have it. The scripture tells us that the unearned nature of God's grace destroys our insecurities.

God's unconditional love breaks the chains of imposter syndrome because His love fosters a sense of security in His grace. I know some of you are struggling with this issue, but as I have told myself and others, you are not an imposter. Where you are right now is where you are supposed to be. If you are in a boardroom feeling you shouldn't be there, or if you are in a bathroom trying to get the nerve up to enter a space, you feel overwhelmed, chin up, back straight, and walk like the child of God you are. Find strength and confidence through Christ.

Reflection:

_____

_____

_____

_____

_____

_____

_____

_____

_____

_____

_____

_____

_____

_____

_____

_____

_____

_____

_____

_____

_____

6

Embracing Change: How to Trust God's New Things - Reflection

I expect God to do something new and exciting in my life every year. When we expect it, we can trust it will happen. However, only some people expect change or embrace it. Change and the unknown frighten people. The thought of change is scary to some and exhausting to others. I get that. But to me, change is what makes the world go round. Change is the thing that moves us from the status quo to the next level, and instead of resisting it, I welcome it.

One of my favorite sayings is attributed to Mahatma Gandhi. "Be the change you want to see in the world." Unfortunately, many want to see things change but need more time to step into it. In the Bible, Joshua had to assume a leadership role after Moses died. As great as he was, he dealt with fear. God reminded Joshua four times to "be strong and courageous."

An earlier story about Joshua is when Moses sent twelve spies into Canaan to see if they could take it. Ten returned with news that the land was prosperous and great! However, the bad news they reported was that they could not take it because men of great stature filled it and would devour them. However, a courageous Joshua and his friend Caleb had a different report and a different outlook. Instead of being fearful, do you know what they said? "If the Lord delights in us, then He will bring us into this land and give it to us!" I love that attitude.

Reading these words made me ponder life and my part in it. Every day, we have an opportunity to make an impact. We can follow God as He leads us into new territory. I want my attitude to be just like Caleb's and Joshua's. "If the Lord delights in us, then He will give it to us."

I am confident He will give us a glimpse of what could be if we only take a step toward it. I want to encourage you to let your dreams and goals be so big that everyone will know that it must have been God when they are accomplished. That's how I live my life; going after the dreams God gives me and trusting that He will help me achieve them.

I get excited when something big comes to mind because I automatically think that God is doing something new. So as I tell myself, "I say to you, 'Don't look back at the old or get bogged down with the past.'" Perceive the new thing He wants to do in your life. And remember Isaiah 43:18–19 when you begin to question. "Forget the former things; do not dwell on the past. See, I am doing a new thing! Now it springs up; do you not perceive it? I am making a way in the desert and streams in the wasteland."

Reflection:

_____

_____

_____

_____

_____

_____

_____

_____

_____

_____

_____

_____

_____

_____

_____

_____

_____

_____

_____

_____

_____

7

Embracing Authenticity: Unveiling the Power of Psalm 139:14

Life's journey often takes us through peaks and valleys, challenging us to discover our true selves amid the chaos. The Bible offers profound wisdom and solace in times of doubt and self-discovery. One such verse, Psalm 139:14, beautifully reminds us that we are "fearfully and wonderfully made." This declaration holds the power to transform the way we perceive ourselves and our purpose. The inspiration this scripture brings causes us to look at our unique selves and how we can lead a more fulfilling and impactful life.

First, recognize God's handiwork by reflecting on the profound truth that we are creations of a loving God. Just as an artist pours their heart into their masterpiece, so too has God intricately woven every fiber of our being. Embracing this truth allows us to find beauty in our flaws, strength in our weaknesses, and purpose in every aspect of our lives. Each of us is a masterpiece, and our individuality is a testament to the Creator's infinite creativity.

Second, we can overcome self-doubt. In a world that often magnifies our imperfections, it's easy to fall into the trap of self-doubt. But when we internalize the message of Psalm 139:14, we're reminded that we are fearfully and wonderfully made. Our uniqueness isn't a cause for shame or insecurity; it's a reason to celebrate. Embracing our strengths and acknowledging our weaknesses with humility allows us to grow and evolve into the best versions of ourselves.

Third, as we learn to embrace our authentic selves, we free ourselves from the pressure to conform to societal norms or others' expectations. Embracing our authentic selves empowers us to pursue our passions, voice our opinions, and contribute to the world in ways only we can. Our individuality becomes a source of inspiration for others seeking to break free from the shackles of conformity.

Fourth, we can cultivate self-love and compassion by seeing ourselves as God sees us. By recognizing our worth, we open the door to self-love and compassion. Just as the Creator loves us unconditionally, we can learn to love ourselves despite our flaws. This self-love becomes a wellspring of confidence allowing us to face challenges with resilience and grace. Additionally, as we learn to love ourselves, we extend that love to others, fostering a sense of unity and empathy in our relationships.

Fifth, discovering our purpose is a journey that often requires introspection and self-discovery. Our purpose becomes more apparent when we believe we are fearfully and wonderfully made. We are called to use our talents, passions, and experiences to impact the world around us positively. Whether our purpose is found in our careers, relationships, or community service, embracing our uniqueness empowers us to pursue our calling with unwavering dedication.

Psalm 139:14 constantly reminds us that we are fearfully and wonderfully made. This affirmation can transform our lives by helping us recognize our inherent worth, embrace authenticity, and pursue our unique purpose. As we journey through life, let's hold onto this truth, drawing strength from the knowledge that we are cherished creations of a loving Creator. By doing so, we can inspire others to walk confidently in their own unique identities and leave an indelible mark on the world.

Reflection:

_____

_____

_____

_____

_____

_____

_____

_____

_____

_____

_____

_____

_____

_____

_____

_____

_____

_____

_____

_____

8

Renewing the Mind: Finding Peace and Self-Approval

Have you ever walked into a room and felt you didn't belong? I understand. I can recall entering meetings and feeling that nobody wanted me there. The glances, looks, or furrowed brows graced the faces of some people present. When I was young, these looks, spiraled me into a series of negative thoughts. I have never thought of myself as not good enough, but I have felt that others deemed me unworthy of acknowledgement. During those times, I sometimes struggled to bring my attention to the purpose of the meeting because of their looks.

Perceived rejection is a terrible thing to deal with. Perceived rejection is assuming rejection before it has happened. Some people are geniuses at prerejecting themselves on someone else's behalf. These same folks will interpret the squint of the eyes as disapproval and the purse of the lips as annoyance toward them; they assume they are already rejected. Therefore, they embrace behavior that leads them into a cycle of rejecting themselves and others to protect themselves.

Why do you think falling prey to unfit feelings and destructive behaviors is so easy? If God says we are made in His perfect image, why do we automatically accept that we are not good enough? I'll tell you why. It's the human condition! When we get stuck in patterns of prerejection, we wrestle with these. We assume the worst about ourselves and others. Our focus drills inward until we see ourselves through a rejected lens. It takes us down the path of assumptions, leading to misunderstandings and broken relationships. God wants us to know who we are in Christ—chosen, approved, desired, and disciplined. Yet we readily accept the opposite about ourselves because of the reactions from others.

While many of us have external struggles, we also deal with internal battles. The mind is one of the most incredible places of conflict, where internal battles are won or lost, and prerejection steals our peace and promotes anxious thoughts, influencing our actions and attitudes. Remember all these thoughts and conflicts are being waged in our minds and seen in our attitudes and actions. So we must start with our minds to overcome these feelings of rejection.

Romans 12:2 tells us to "be transformed by the renewal of our minds." Paul encouraged the Philippians to guard their hearts. Protecting our hearts promotes peace within ourselves and our relationships, but just like anything else, we must put in the effort. Our minds naturally run along negative tracks, but we can retrain our thoughts.

Start by looking for the good in others. Realize when you assume that someone has rejected you, you may be projecting your fear of rejection onto them. They might be frowning in your direction not because of you but because of something in their life.

Do I still experience anxiety in spaces where people don't like me? Yep, I do. Do I shut down, close off, and reject them? Sometimes. I am still working on myself.

Reflection:

_____

_____

_____

_____

_____

_____

_____

_____

_____

_____

_____

_____

_____

_____

_____

_____

_____

_____

_____

_____

9

Embracing Confidence and Consistency: Lessons from Proverbs and Philippians

Have you ever looked at some people who just seemed to exude confidence? Yeah, I have, too. Have you ever wondered why some folks have no problem stepping up and taking on any challenge without worries while others shy away? Are you one of those who lacks confidence and privately wonder why you cannot overcome the fear of not being "good enough"? Also, when does self-confidence become arrogance?

There are so many questions with one answer. It all begins with God. If you start with God as your foundation, you will surely build self-confidence rather than arrogance. How would you know? The Holy Spirit will remind you.

Now how do you build confidence? It begins with God also. The first thing that comes to mind is the scripture that reminds us that we are made in God's image. Another one says, "I can do all things through Christ who gives me strength." And another tells us, "God's gifts and calling are irrevocable." So if you begin with what the Word of God says about you and fill your mind with these things rather than the harmful noise, you can build confidence.

I want to emphasize the profound significance of believing in yourself, staying the course, and embracing confidence and consistency on the journey to success. As we navigate life's challenges, a timeless wisdom is found in scripture that resonates with these principles.

Proverbs 3:5–6 reminds us to "trust in the Lord with all our hearts and lean not on our understanding." This scripture is a foundation for self-belief, urging us to believe in our abilities even when faced with uncertainties. The path to success often requires us to trust our capabilities, but I reject that. We must trust God first and then believe He cares about the things that concern us and will help us achieve our dreams and goals.

As we go through life, we will face obstacles, but faith, perseverance, and resilience can lead to eventual success. Staying true to our goals, even in the face of adversity, is a testament to God's power working through us.

Confidence and consistency find a voice in Philippians 4:13. "I can do all things through Christ who strengthens me." This verse highlights the empowerment that comes from a confident belief in God and confidence in oneself, coupled with the consistency of effort. Remember our abilities are amplified when rooted in faith and sustained through dedicated, consistent action.

As you pursue your aspirations, remember to draw inspiration from the scriptures. They emphasize belief, perseverance, and confidence. Remember by believing in ourselves, staying the course, and being confident and consistent, we unlock the door to a future where success is not just a destination but a journey of growth and fulfillment.

Reflection:

_____

_____

_____

_____

_____

_____

_____

_____

_____

_____

_____

_____

_____

_____

_____

_____

_____

_____

_____

_____

10

The Impact of Stress on Our Bodies: A Personal Account

Being sick stinks, and as healthy as we try to keep ourselves, sometimes illness just latches on. When I get sick, I usually don't stop. I just keep pushing myself until my body says, "No more." Then I am in bed for days, trying to get better and wondering, *Why? What now?* And all the above.

Do you ask yourself the same questions? When an illness comes out of nowhere, do you wonder, *How did I get here? What did I miss?* For me, I am extra careful. I run six days a week and eat healthy, but I somehow missed something. The more my thoughts wander trying to pinpoint why I got sick, I cannot help but think back to when I was profoundly ill in 2012. I retired in November 2011, and in December, I fell sick and did not recover for an entire year.

I wonder if my body had warned me back then and I failed to listen. Has your body been telling you something that you may be ignoring? Why do we give little thought to the small and big life stresses? Why do we discount the toll mental or emotional stress can have on our bodies?

When I quietly and peacefully waited for God to heal me, I did everything necessary to take care of my body. One thing

I never stopped doing was reading my Bible. The scripture in Philippians 4:6–7 came to mind.

> Be anxious for nothing, but in all things through prayer and supplication with thanksgiving, let your requests be made known unto God. And the peace of God, which passes all understanding, will guard your hearts and minds through Christ Jesus.

What does this mean in the context of stress in any area of our lives? It means, "Don't sweat the small stuff." I learned this scripture many years ago, but I constantly need help to live it out daily. Why can't I just let things go? Why am I sometimes obsessed with control and ensuring every detail goes right? I am sure God knows I am this way and forgives me when I falter. However, I need to learn to forgive myself, forgive others, and release any anxiety I hold over any uncontrollable situation I face.

I don't know about you, but whatever you may face at home, at work, or in your community, if something gets to you, learn to breathe, take a walk, and repeat to yourself that you are casting your anxieties on God because you know He doesn't want you sick physically, mentally, or emotionally. He cares for you.

Remember to pray while you wait for God to show you how to release the pressure of stress in your life.

Reflection:

_____

_____

_____

_____

_____

_____

_____

_____

_____

_____

_____

_____

_____

_____

_____

_____

_____

_____

_____

11

Embracing Life with Faith and Purpose: A Reflection

We are blessed with the gift of life, with divine purpose and intention. Life is meant to be lived positively and purposefully; we should embrace every moment with gratitude and determination. Despite our challenges, we should cast aside blame and excuses, for they only hinder our progress.

Instead, let us embrace ownership of our lives, recognizing that we can shape our destiny through our thoughts, words, and actions. Remember what Philippians 4:13 says. "I can do all things through him who strengthens me." With faith as our guide and God's grace as our strength, there is nothing we cannot overcome.

Each day, let us reflect on Jesus Christ's ultimate act of love and sacrifice on the cross. His resurrection symbolizes hope, renewal, and the promise of new beginnings. Let this remind us that no matter how difficult our circumstances may seem, there is always hope on the horizon.

As followers of Christ, we know that our faith fuels hope. One such scripture reminds us, "Faith is the confidence of what we hope for the assurance of what we cannot see (Hebrews 11:11). We hope, expect, and have confidence in God to do what He promises in His Word. Do you know what those promises are? If not, I will share a few so that you can recall them when needed. When the enemy tells you are defeated, you can say, "No, I am not, because this is what God promised:

- "He promises to never leave me (Hebrews 13:5),
- "He promises to send me a Comforter to counsel and help me (John 15:26),
- "He promises to strengthen me (Isaiah 41:10), and
- "He promises to meet my needs. (Philippians 4:19)."

I encourage you to embrace your life wholeheartedly. Seize each day with courage and conviction, knowing that the One who created you loves you unconditionally. I pray that you will allow faith, positivity, and purpose to drive your actions, for in doing so, you will unlock the full potential of your God-given talents.

Reflection:

_____

_____

_____

_____

_____

_____

_____

_____

_____

_____

_____

_____

_____

_____

_____

_____

_____

_____

_____

_____

12

Embracing Gentleness: The Power of Softening Our Words

As someone who has long believed in the direct approach, I've come to understand the importance of softening our words and embracing gentleness in our communication.

In a world where candor and straightforwardness are often celebrated, it's easy to overlook the impact our words can have on others. The truth is our words have the power to either build up or tear down as well as to inspire or to wound. And in the pursuit of being direct, we sometimes forget the profound effect our tone and delivery can have on those around us.

The Bible offers wisdom, reminding us that "gentle words turn away wrath, but a harsh word stirs up anger" (Proverbs 15:1). My grandfather used to say, "To make friends, show yourself friendly." That's biblical, too. See Proverbs 18:24.

This simple yet profound truth underscores the transformative power of gentleness in our interactions. When we approach others with gentleness, we not only disarm hostility but also create an environment of understanding and empathy.

Gentleness does not imply weakness or timidity; rather, it signifies strength under control. It takes courage to temper our words, to choose kindness over bluntness, and to prioritize the well-being of others above our desire to be heard. Moreover, gentleness fosters deeper connections and strengthens relationships. When we communicate with gentleness, we convey respect, humility, and a genuine concern for the feelings of others. It allows us to navigate conflicts with grace and resolve differences with compassion.

Our goal should be to cultivate gentleness in our speech and actions and to remember that it is not about diluting our message or compromising our values. Instead, it is about infusing our interactions with warmth, empathy, and understanding.

Today and the days to follow, let us embrace gentleness as a guiding principle in our communication. Let's recognize its transformative power to diffuse tension, foster connection, and cultivate harmony in our personal and professional relationships. May we always remember the absolute truth, the Word of God, that gentle words turn away wrath and have the extraordinary ability to sow seeds of peace.

Reflection:

_____

_____

_____

_____

_____

_____

_____

_____

_____

_____

_____

_____

_____

_____

_____

_____

_____

_____

_____

_____

_____

13

Navigating Leadership Challenges: A Journey of Reflection

I have faced my ups and downs over the years. I have had to make unpleasant decisions that affected other people's lives, and I have repeatedly confronted my shortcomings. I don't care how old one is; facing our shortcomings is hard. Genuinely looking inward makes us so vulnerable.

I have been in leadership from the very beginning of my work career. After graduating from college, I landed a job in a management training program with the federal government. I have experience in various levels and positions in leadership, which has also been my area of study in both my doctoral programs. As a result of work experiences and study, I tend to have very high expectations of people holding leadership roles. My expectations can be exhilarating for some and exhausting for others. Dare I say to some people my expectations can make them feel less than adequate.

My leadership style has been called into question more than once. I recall a person I was holding accountable state that because I asked him why in several instances, I made him feel "unsafe" and "demoralized." I was baffled! More than that, I felt insulted. I thought about that exchange for days. I even prayed about it. Although I prayed, I could not shake his comments. His comments bothered me.

I revisited the meeting in my mind and recalled his posture as I sat there and listened to him. In several instances, I felt he was passive-aggressive. I was sure he purposefully used trigger words to disarm me and to come in for the kill. As he spoke, all I could think about was how he misrepresented certain situations we had discussed. He was gaslighting me, and for days, his words stuck with me no matter how hard I tried to shake them off. I kept telling myself to reflect Christ, but my anxiety and frustration were getting the best of me.

I have always felt that as distance happens between an event and you, you feel the pain less. After several days, I could stop and take a good look at myself. I asked myself, "Am I purposefully trying to demoralize anyone?" "Do I try to intimidate?" My answer was an emphatic no. However, I did learn from that situation that I am still growing. I get hurt like everyone else when others misunderstand my words or actions.

I believe God's grace bridges our shortcomings. The Word of God says, "His mercies are new every morning. Great is thy faithfulness." At some point, we will all face conflict. We will all be misunderstood. We can sit and stew in misunderstandings or look at them as opportunities for growth. I intend to do the latter. We can also hold a grudge, but as a follower of Christ, I will choose to try to reflect His image every day.

Reflection:

_____

_____

_____

_____

_____

_____

_____

_____

_____

_____

_____

_____

_____

_____

_____

_____

_____

_____

_____

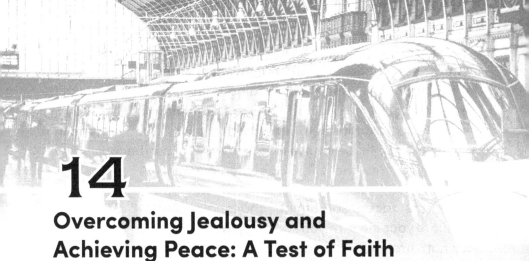

14

Overcoming Jealousy and Achieving Peace: A Test of Faith

I begin each year with a spiritual fast. As I fast and pray, I ask God to help me be kinder, gentler, and more compassionate. It sounds corny, but a straightforward person like me can be seen as tough and challenging. The truth is I am also kind and understanding.

As I reflect, my mind goes to a saying I would hear as a child. "Don't be surprised when you come under attack. There's always some test right before your breakthrough." OK, but I do not expect many of the challenges I have faced from those close to me. I am thinking of a particular challenge I faced one year.

As I faced the issue, I wanted to lash out. I was furious, and when I was mad, anything could happen. I remember thinking, *I have been there for that person. There's no way they will let anyone or anything overshadow how much I care for them and have been there for them.* When I thought the foolishness had settled, I learned later that it had not. I was furious again. However, somewhere along the way, God brought me peace. When conversations occurred regarding this issue, I noticed I did not react anymore. I felt a sense of calm.

Today, I can confidently say that my calm came from that time of fasting, prayer, and Bible reading. Although the scriptures I read during the month had nothing to do with peace, today, I think of the scripture in Isaiah 26:3 that says, "You will keep in perfect peace those whose minds are steadfast, because they trust in you." Yes, that's it. God settled my mind.

Have you faced something challenging lately? Stop and evaluate your life. Are you succeeding at something that others are not? Are your wins secretly infuriating others? How do you know? We have all been at the point of exasperation when we encounter situations that we had no idea were simmering under the surface. If you don't know that someone has deep resentment toward you, how do you handle it when it finally rises to the surface? It's hard.

Attacks can be physical, emotional, mental, or spiritual. It's unfortunate when we don't see them coming, and it is even more challenging to be confronted and not know how to respond. One underlying reason people attack is their insecurities; they may have secret jealousies you never knew existed. But when you win and continue to do so, you stir up their jealousy. Guess what? You have no control over their thoughts or their insecurities. People may smile in your face the entire time, hoping to see you fail. When you don't, they find ways to get to you.

Today, let me encourage you to let God bring peace and calm when someone injects chaos. Pray for those who despitefully use you, and don't regret trusting those who may betray you. Do not let those against you stop you from loving, living, and being all God has called you to be. If their attacks stop you, they win. Remember you are blessed and highly favored. Don't let anyone cause you to question that. Don't put your head down. Don't sulk, and do not stop what you are doing to make them happy. Head up, shoulders back, and keep winning.

Reflection:

_____

_____

_____

_____

_____

_____

_____

_____

_____

_____

_____

_____

_____

_____

_____

_____

_____

_____

_____

_____

_____

_____

15

God's Irrevocable Gifts: Overcoming Doubt and Limitations

For many years, I have talked repeatedly and positively about how God uniquely calls each of us. I have preached that everyone should recognize that and never let anyone take that away. I have even cautioned others not to allow the enemy to convince you that you are less valuable.

After all the years of saying that to others and myself, I sometimes question my calling. Why is that? Why do the most confident people ask if they have unique talents? I'll tell you why. It's because when we do not use it or feel that we fail at whatever we initially thought was that gift, our humanness causes us to question.

When we know we heard from God to take a job, to move to another city and start a ministry, to step out and sing, or the thousands of other things I know He has given people, we doubt. Initially the excitement sets in and we are rearing to go. However, after the initial exhilaration, we begin to question. That questioning of oneself turns into talking ourselves out of what we know to be true. We talk ourselves out of what we heard. That's the doubt, which is the enemy's potent weapon. But remember when God calls us, He will equip us!

In times past, I have said that each calling looks different. The unique gifts God has given you are for you, and the ones He has given me are for me. Maybe you don't feel there is anything special about you. You may think God blessed others with unique talents but not you. I want to gently remind you of the scripture in Romans 11:29. "For the gifts and the calling of God are irrevocable (for He does not withdraw what He has given, nor does He change His mind about those to whom He gives His call)."

The next time you feel down or allow someone to put limitations on you, repeat that scripture to yourself. Also remember Eleanor Roosevelt's words. "No one can make you feel inferior without your consent." So please don't give it to them.

Reflection:

_____

_____

_____

_____

_____

_____

_____

_____

_____

_____

_____

_____

_____

_____

_____

_____

_____

_____

_____

16

Navigating Attacks with Faith: Overcoming Fear and Finding Strength in the Word of God

All my life, I have heard the phrase "Be kind. You never know what someone might be going through." I believe people think of a particular type when they use this statement. They do not think of people like me. They do not think that a confident, educated person, and what some see as successful, is going through anything; they don't think someone like me needs others to be kind. But I do! I do because I, just like you, face attacks.

Confident people try hard to hold life together for themselves and others. Early in life, we are taught that we can handle anything. We have somehow bought into the narrative "What does not kill you makes you stronger." We are taught to stand up in the face of controversy and not allow others to get to us. The truth is people like me get tired of standing and fighting our battles in quiet only to be attacked in public. That's no fun at all.

Lately I have faced the cruel reality that sometimes when people seem OK, they are not. I am not a naive person, and I have lived long enough to know that everyone and everything may not be what they present to others, but it is still shocking to the system when you come face-to-face with this reality. To go head-to-head with people you respect is no fun. I found myself in the middle of a war. The situation was so irrational that I honestly did not know how to navigate erratic behavior, disruption, and personal attacks. I wanted to lash out but had to think about professional comportment and spiritual responsibility. Aren't I supposed to turn the other cheek? Am I supposed to fight back?

Jesus told us to turn the other cheek. Matthew 5:38–42 NKJV says,

> You have heard that it was said, An eye for an eye and a tooth for a tooth. But I say to you, do not resist the one who is evil. But if anyone slaps you on the right cheek, turn to him the other also. And if anyone wants to sue you and take your shirt, hand over your coat as well. If anyone forces you to go one mile, go with them two miles. Give to the one who asks you, and do not turn away from the one who wants to borrow from you.

Oh wow. That's pretty clear.

So many Bible passages tell me not to worry because God's got me covered. He has often told me not to be a coward but to be courageous and not lose heart. However, when I must face evil, my spirit faints. I shake at the core, and my anxiety level goes through the roof!

Yet I have also noticed that those moments when I am scared only last a little while. I run to the Word for support as soon as I get my footing. The Word of God fuels my faith, and I am ready for the next thing. I tell myself, "I can do all things through Christ who strengthens me." I remind myself of Joshua 1:9, which says, "Be strong and courageous; do not be frightened or dismayed, for the Lord your God is with you wherever you go." Or Deuteronomy 31:6–8 NKJV, which says, "Be strong and bold; have no fear or dread of them because the Lord your God goes before you. He will be with you; he will not fail you or forsake you."

You see, there are many scriptures of support in the Word of God. The more I repeat them to myself, the more I feel my strength rising. I can see my countenance change from anxiety, defeat, and cowardice to courage, confidence, and calm, trusting that He is with me whatever I face and He will defend me.

What battles are you fighting today? What person or situation has you up at night wondering what you will do or how you will handle your next attack? Instead of worrying about the person or thing, turn your worry into worship. Join me as I stop worrying about what someone might say or do to try to hurt me and start thanking God for protecting me where He placed me for the time He has called me.

Reflection:

_____

_____

_____

_____

_____

_____

_____

_____

_____

_____

_____

_____

_____

_____

_____

_____

17

Rushing versus God's Will: A Runner's Reflection

Philippians 4:6–7

As I readied myself for my morning run, I checked the temperature outside to find it was supposed to be a pleasant fifty-one degrees. That's warm weather when you are a runner! So instead of putting on layers of long-sleeved shirts, I put on what I thought would be suitable for my run: a tank top, a thin, cotton shirt, and a little jacket. The minute the garage opened and I was on the other side, I could feel the chilly air. "Boy, I thought it would be warmer," I said to myself. However cold I felt, I refused to go back inside to change and just kept to my scheduled run.

While my feet hit the pavement, I ran up the hill and immediately noticed the flashing lights. The closer I got, I could see a truck was on top of the median facing me and a tow truck was on the opposite side, blocking the departing traffic while adjusting to a position to tow the vehicle.

As I ran down the hill, away from the vehicles, I tried not to look but found myself locking eyes with the distressed vehicle driver and the tow truck driver. I looked away and kept running, yet I noticed only one or two cars waiting for the tow truck to clear the path. When I got down the hill and began my trek back up, as I approached the vehicle and tow truck, I noticed that many backed-up cars were waiting and probably trying to get to work.

I wonder what happened. Several times, I have seen folks lose control and crash on that median. I have seen people speed on that hill as if they were on a motor speedway. I wonder what was so urgent this particular morning for this man. I would not be honest if I said that I hadn't done my share of speeding up and down that mountain. But when I see the flashing slow-down sign, I am jolted into realizing how fast I am going and slow down to the forty-five-miles-per-hour sign.

Seeing this guy made me think about us rushing to get where we were going. Today's society is about getting it done and not wasting time, especially in the Western world. We say, "Time is money," "Don't waste my time," or "Lead, follow, or get out of the way!" We have no time for those who waste it. Yet I think we are correct when we rush to get something done when maybe that's the opposite of what God wants from us.

Suppose God wants us to stop, listen, and then move once we are sure what we are rushing to accomplish is aligned with His will for our lives. What if we are running in a direction opposite from where He wants us to be?

Perhaps the answer lies in Philippians 4:6–7.

> Be anxious for nothing, but in everything by prayer and supplication, with thanksgiving, let your requests be made known to God; and the peace of God, which surpasses all understanding, will guard your hearts and minds through Christ Jesus.

Reflection:

_____

_____

_____

_____

_____

_____

_____

_____

_____

_____

_____

_____

_____

_____

_____

_____

_____

_____

_____

_____

_____

_____

18

Overcoming Challenges with Hope: Finding Joy in the Present

The older I get, the more aware I am of how much time I might have left on this earth. However, the last several years brought it home. Not only did we live in isolation during the first year of the pandemic, thinking by the end of the year we would emerge happy and healthy, but we also entered a second year with the same challenges that kept us guarded and somewhat isolated as the year before. Then just when we thought we were coming out of a pandemic, variations of a virus we all came to know as COVID-19 began to show up in the forms of Delta and Omicron, among others. Our lives started to unravel again as we had to return to measures that had already exhausted us.

In addition to the pandemic, we had to deal with other issues of life that could have quickly taken away our hope, and for me, the last year brought about traumatic matters. Friends I loved and cared about deeply, without any warning, were no longer here. How could that be? Angel was only twenty-eight; Melanie was not even fifty! Mike was still playing music and maybe sixty! The hardest thing for me was to find out by accident that someone I heard from regularly stopped responding, and I learned they, too, were gone: my dear friends Valerie and Maureen. The loss of these precious friends and unique relationships caused the reality of how uncertain our time is here. I still don't think I have recovered yet. Anytime I experience a series of losses, I start to reflect on my mortality. I wonder if you do also.

Mortality is hard to face, yet we all must meet it someday. I do not want to bring a sad and depressing message. Instead, I want to offer hope. I want to remind you that today is yours if you are blessed to see it. Tomorrow is not promised; we never know when it may be our last. And no matter what tomorrow holds, just be assured that God has tomorrow. He also offers hope. Despite all that happened during the previous years, what I remember most are the beautiful things that happened in my life. I got a new job, another degree, a new home, and new friends. See? Even when we go through stuff that makes us feel helpless, we must look for the other things God sends along the way. I bet you will find that you experienced as many beautiful things as you did of the others.

Whenever you need to lift yourself out of a funk, turn to the one source that offers hope to the hopeless, peace to the unsettled, and joy amid sadness. Do not look to your surroundings to be joyful; you will be lost. Look to God. Psalm 42:5–6 reads,

> Why are you cast down, O my soul, why are you in turmoil within me? Hope in God; for I shall again praise Him, my salvation and my God.

The psalmist says, "I don't care what state I find myself in, and right now it is in total despair; God is still my hope."

For any challenges you face, hold on to scripture that gives you hope. Tell yourself, "Today is the day the Lord has made; I will rejoice and be glad." Be intentional in the way you embrace the day. Someone may need you to lift them.

Reflection:

_____

_____

_____

_____

_____

_____

_____

_____

_____

_____

_____

_____

_____

_____

_____

_____

_____

_____

_____

_____

19

Cultivating Gratitude Daily: The Transformative Power of Thankfulness

It should come as no surprise that I believe in the power of thankfulness and our need to focus on gratitude. Gratitude is something we take for granted.

What I mean is that it feels superficial when we wait for the Thanksgiving holiday to focus on it. To me, every single day that we are alive is a day to be grateful. Family members and even relationships with old friends are reasons to be thankful.

What is gratitude, and why do we need to have it? There are two kinds of gratitude. Both are important, but I want to focus on biblical gratitude. One author wrote that biblical gratitude means giving others goodness and grace, as we have received from God. It means to extend the joy of receiving to others and God through gestures of kindness and goodness. It is what Galatians 5:22–23 says. "But the fruit of the Spirit is love, joy, peace, forbearance, kindness, goodness, faithfulness, gentleness, and self-control."

I trust that when we extend these gifts to others, we get them in return. I also believe that the only way we can genuinely exercise these fruits is to start by recognizing that all of these are extended to us by the grace of God. As such, we should be thankful that He thought enough of us to extend them. Some might ask, "How did He do that?" Through His Son, Jesus. John 3:16 tells us, "For God so loved the world, that he gave his only Son, that whoever believes in him should not perish but have eternal life."

You might be unable to wrap your mind around these scriptures, and I can understand that. People have asked me how I can believe them. Well, I'll tell you how: through faith. Faith that when I give, I will receive. When I forgive, others will forgive me. When I show grace to others, people will extend that same grace to me. For that, I am grateful.

I genuinely believe that gratitude tends to eliminate cynicism, sarcasm, and mistrust. A thankful heart creates optimism rather than pessimism, and it causes us to give others the benefit of the doubt.

Reflection:

_____

_____

_____

_____

_____

_____

_____

_____

_____

_____

_____

_____

_____

_____

_____

_____

_____

_____

_____

_____

FINAL THOUGHTS

I indeed can find a lot to look back on with dread. Like you, I can regret everything that took place, whether personal anxieties, professional obstacles, or career setbacks. I can complain or be thankful for what did not happen. There were times over the years that I must confess I did not know what to do. I just took one day at a time, refused to let fear control me, kept trying to do my responsible part, and continued to live.

As I finish this book of reflections, I think about things I have said to myself since I was young. I think about the books I have written, and what has struck me most was the title of one of those books. *It's Your Life, Own It. No Blame. No Excuses* is one that I reflect on most because never has a title meant more to me over the years.

At the beginning of 2020, a few months before the pandemic hit, I knew it would be a year of change for me. I loved my job but not the environment. I realized that no matter how much I tried, my values did not align with those of others. I decided that I could stay and become more miserable every day or leave at a good place on my terms. I decided to do the latter, even though I did not know what I would do next.

I had just sold my house and moved into a lease that would keep me in the area for one year. Almost immediately after I resigned, I went home, and the state went into lockdown. So talk about uncertainty and second-guessing myself. During that month in quarantine, I read a lot, played on the internet, and rested. Also during that month, my mind played games with me. *Did I make the right decision? What now? Maybe I should have given it more time.* And similar thoughts. Do you know what I did when that would happen? I would remind myself that I had prayed about my life, thoroughly thought through my decision, decided, and had to own it. *The end.*

Whew! Doing what I did could be somewhat disturbing and certainly anxiety-ridden for anyone. However, what could I have done about the decision I had already made? I could not reverse it so I had to live with it. I could do one or two things: sit and sweat it, dread what I had done, and worry about a choice I had made, thereby ensuring I would live in a state of negativity each day, or I could embrace my decision. I could look to the future, believe I had done the right thing, and be open to what was next.

I share my story not to brag on me but to help you see that your life is yours and attitude means everything. Do not allow what the crowd may say about the economy to stop you. Do not let what your family may tell you about your limitations limit you. Please do not allow what you tell yourself about how others see or treat you to become your self-talk. Believe that your future is yours. Trust that you have what it takes and take the steps you need to achieve what you desire.

Never forget God along your life's journey. I have never stopped believing He has a plan and purpose for me. It would be best if you did not forget that either.

Printed in the United States
by Baker & Taylor Publisher Services